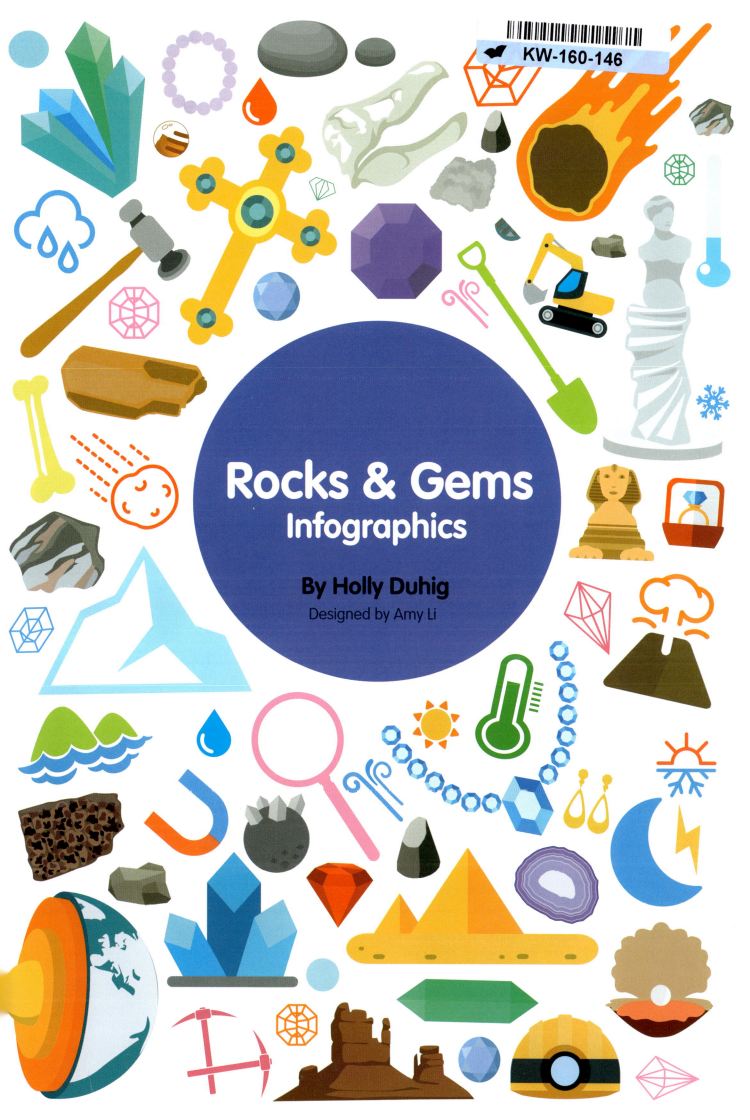

Rocks & Gems
Infographics

By Holly Duhig

Designed by Amy Li

Photo Credits

2 – Lilu330, 4 – David Darko, 6 – OKPic, Mr.Luck, 7 – Designua, NotionPic, Vectors Bang, 8 – Haosame, Visual Generation, Elvetica, 10 – denisik11, Jemastock, 11 – Teguh Mujino, NotionPic, Nadya_Art, 12 – Sentavio, Red monkey, Macrovector, 13 – Mr.Luck, 15 – LuckyVector, 18 – kornilov007, In-Finity, BlueRingMedia, ILeysen, MicroOne, 19 – Lomingo, Vectorpocket, 20 – BlueRingMedia, Lytvynenko Anna, Igor Nazarenko, Lorelyn Medina, DaneeShe, 21 – kavalenkava, MSSA, 22 – lady-luck, BlueRingMedia, Teguh Mujiono, Vertata, John T Takai, 23 – lady-luck, subarashii21, 24 – Chalintra.B, KannaA, 25 – Chalintra.B, Nearbirds, Visual Generation, 26 – lady-luck, ducu59us, Hennadii H, MSSA, robuart, 27 – Natsmith1, angkrit, ideyweb, 28 – Vector Tradition, 29 – kornilov007, 30 – Liliia Hryshchenko, Ciripasca.

Images are courtesy of Shutterstock.com.
With thanks to Getty Images, Thinkstock Photo and iStockphoto.

BookLife
PUBLISHING

©2018
BookLife Publishing
King's Lynn
Norfolk, PE30 4LS

ISBN: 978-1-78637-415-8

Written by:

Holly Duhig

Edited by:

Kirsty Holmes

Designed by:

Amy Li

A catalogue record for this book is available from the British Library.

All facts, statistics, web addresses and URLs in this book were verified as valid and accurate at time of writing. No responsibility for any changes to external websites or references can be accepted by either the author or publisher.

Rocks & Gems

Infographics

Contents

Page 4 What Are Rocks?

Page 6 Types of Rocks

Page 10 Weathering and Erosion

Page 14 Rock and Crystal Structures

Page 16 Crystals

Page 18 Diamonds

Page 20 Gemstones

Page 22 Fossils

Page 24 Ancient Stones

Page 26 Art With Rocks

Page 28 Jewellery

Page 30 Activity

Page 31 Glossary

Page 32 Index

Words that look like <u>this</u> are explained in the glossary on page 31.

What Are Rocks?

Rocks are solid materials that form the surface of the Earth. Rocks are made from minerals. Some rocks, like granite, are hard, while others, like chalk, are soft. Rocks are found on the Earth's surface and in its crust, which is the outermost layer of the planet.

Earth is made up of four layers:

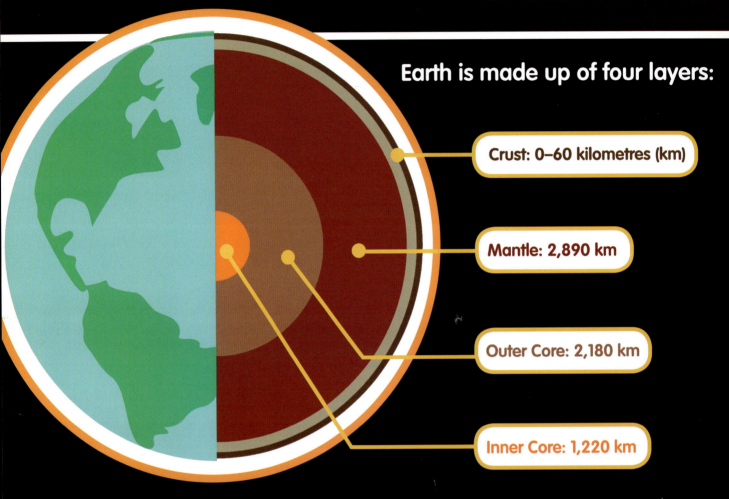

Crust: 0–60 kilometres (km)

Mantle: 2,890 km

Outer Core: 2,180 km

Inner Core: 1,220 km

0–100 km

The Earth's crust is made of solid rock, the mantle is made of semi-molten rock called magma, the outer core is made of liquefied iron, and the inner core is made of solid iron.

The Earth's crust is at its thickest at the top of mountains and at its thinnest under the oceans.

The Earth's crust is split up into giant sections called **tectonic plates.** These float on the magma and move very slowly. When tectonic plates move closer together or farther apart they make beautiful natural formations, such as mountains.

Types of Mountains

Fold Mountains

These are the most common type of mountain. They form when two tectonic plates collide head-on and force the ground upwards.

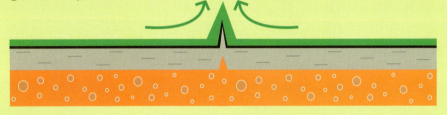

Block Mountains

These form when the Earth's crust fractures or pulls apart.

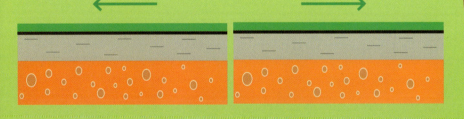

Dome Mountains

These are formed when magma under the Earth's crust pushes upwards creating a smooth bulge in the Earth.

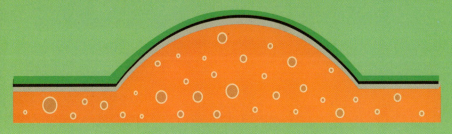

Tectonic plates move very slowly, only moving a few centimetres (cm) per year.

Types of Rocks

There are three main types of rocks: sedimentary, igneous and metamorphic.

Sedimentary Rocks

Sedimentary rocks are formed from tiny pieces of other rocks that have been deposited together. Sedimentary rocks are heavily involved in two processes: **weathering** and **erosion**.

Weathering is the breaking down of rock, and erosion is the moving of the broken down rock elsewhere. Over a long period of time, grains of sand and rock are deposited They build up in layers in a process called sedimentation which causes sedimentary rocks to form.

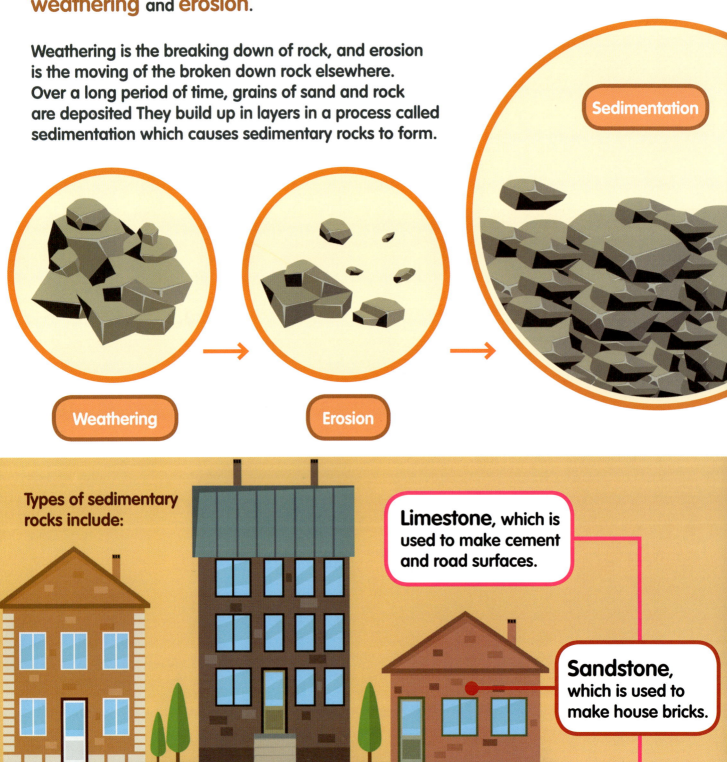

Weathering

Erosion

Sedimentation

Types of sedimentary rocks include:

Limestone, which is used to make cement and road surfaces.

Sandstone, which is used to make house bricks.

Metamorphic Rocks

Metamorphic rocks are rocks that are the result of a underline{transformation} of another rock. Rocks can be transformed because of heat and pressure.

They might have been heated up by the Earth's magma, or buried deep in the Earth under layers of other rock.

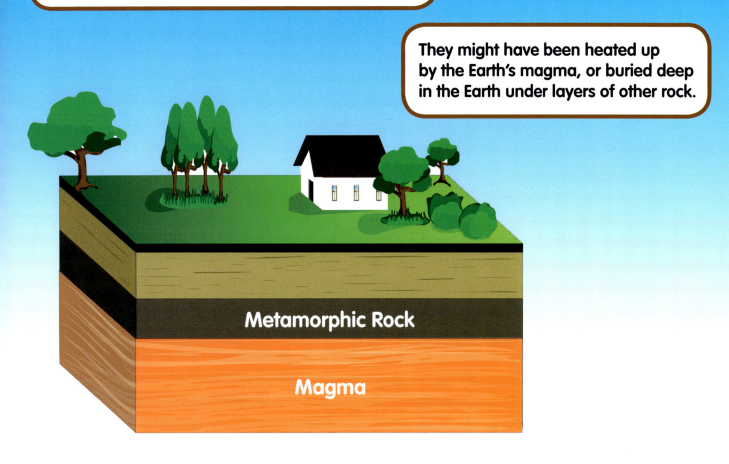

Metamorphic Rock

Magma

Types of metamorphic rocks include:

Slate, which is used to make roof tiles.

Marble, which is used to build famous underline{architecture}, such as the Taj Mahal in India.

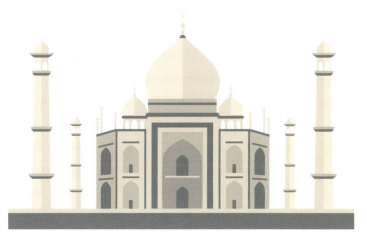

Igneous Rocks

Igneous rocks are rocks that form when magma cools underground or when lava from a volcano cools and solidifies.

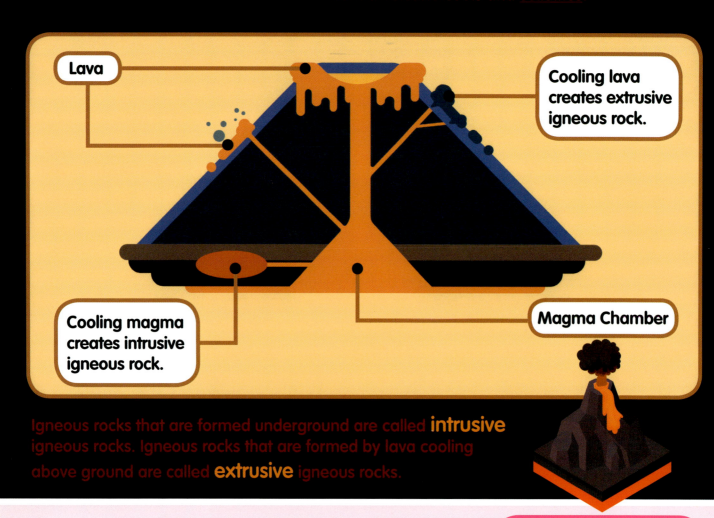

Lava

Cooling lava creates extrusive igneous rock.

Cooling magma creates intrusive igneous rock.

Magma Chamber

Igneous rocks that are formed underground are called **intrusive** igneous rocks. Igneous rocks that are formed by lava cooling above ground are called **extrusive** igneous rocks.

There are **over 700** different kinds of igneous rocks.

Types of igneous rocks include:

Basalt is an extrusive igneous rock which is often used to make massage stones.

Granite is an intrusive igneous rock which is used to make kitchen countertops.

The Giant's Causeway in Ireland is made of **40,000** basalt pillars created by lava cooling and then splitting.

The Rock Cycle

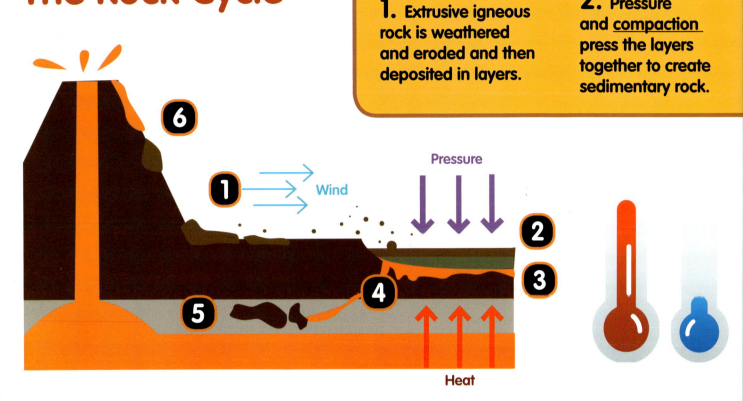

1. Extrusive igneous rock is weathered and eroded and then deposited in layers.

2. Pressure and <u>compaction</u> press the layers together to create sedimentary rock.

Pressure

Wind

Heat

3. More layers get laid down and sedimentary rocks turn into metamorphic rocks due to heat and pressure.

4. Metamorphic rocks get heated so much that they become magma.

5. Some magma cools underground and becomes intrusive igneous rock.

6. Some magma pushes up through the Earth in a volcanic eruption and becomes extrusive igneous rock when it cools.

Types of Rocks in the Earth's Crust:

Sedimentary   Igneous and Metamorphic

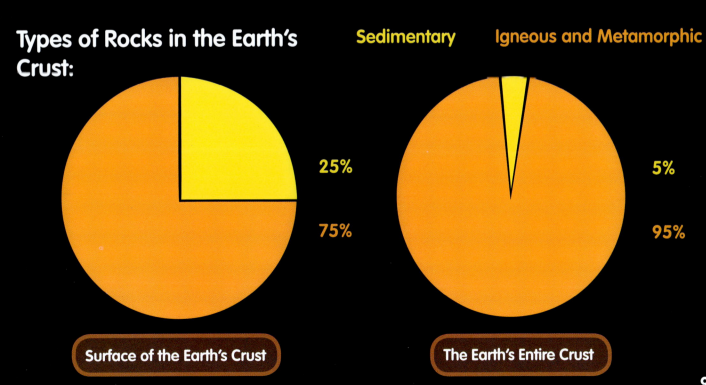

25%

75%

Surface of the Earth's Crust

5%

95%

The Earth's Entire Crust

Weathering and Erosion

Underground Erosion

Some rocks are **porous**, meaning they have plenty of gaps that water can get through. These rocks are often sedimentary rocks, like gypsum and limestone, and are easily weathered by water. As water trickles through rocks underground, it weathers them which causes gaps to form. Over a very long time, these gaps can become **caves**.

Limestone is arranged in layers with horizontal blocks called bedding planes and vertical cracks called joints. This makes it easy for water to get through.

> **Rainwater is slightly <u>acidic</u> which means it can slowly wear away limestone.**

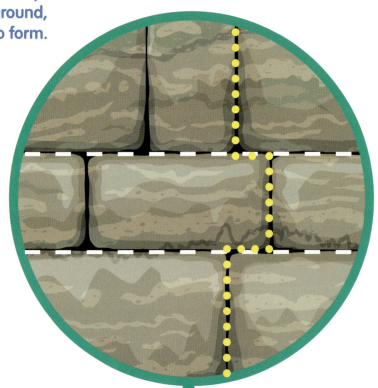

Bedding Planes – – – –	Joints • • • • • • •

The longest cave system in the world is **Mammoth Cave** in Kentucky, USA.

Around 65 km of the cave has been explored so far.

Mammoth Cave Map

Stalactites and Stalagmites

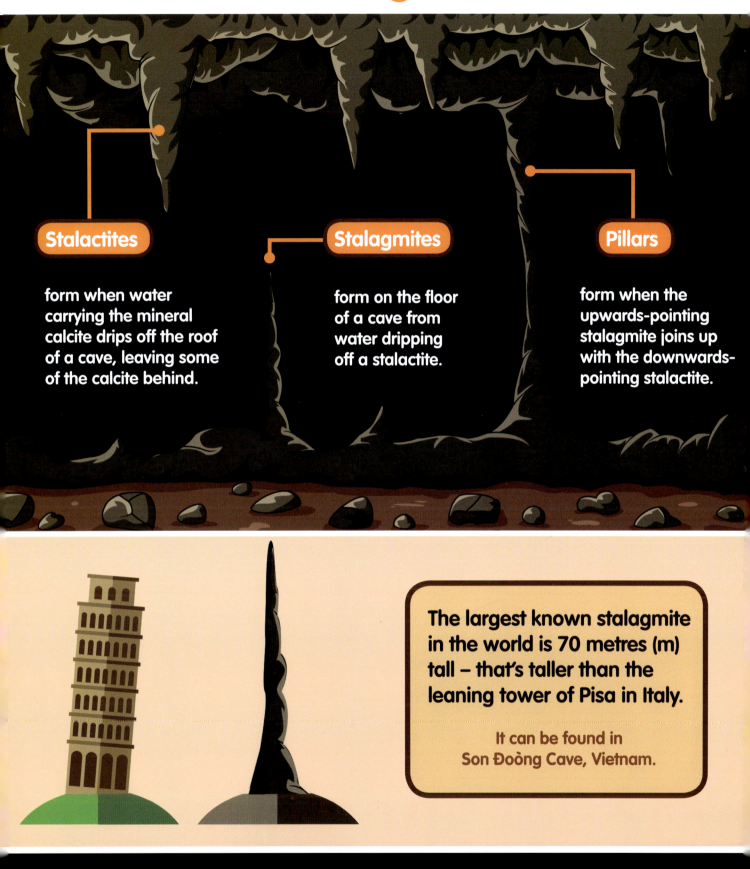

Stalactites

form when water carrying the mineral calcite drips off the roof of a cave, leaving some of the calcite behind.

Stalagmites

form on the floor of a cave from water dripping off a stalactite.

Pillars

form when the upwards-pointing stalagmite joins up with the downwards-pointing stalactite.

The largest known stalagmite in the world is 70 metres (m) tall – that's taller than the leaning tower of Pisa in Italy.

It can be found in Son Đoòng Cave, Vietnam.

The Mulu Caves in Borneo are home to the largest cave chambers and passages on the planet. Deer Chamber is so big that it could fit five cathedrals the size of Saint Paul's in London inside of it

River and Coastal Erosion

The Grand Canyon

The Grand Canyon in Arizona, USA, is a <u>canyon</u> carved by the Colorado River. The Colorado River has weathered and eroded the rock in the Grand Canyon over six million years. The layers of rock exposed by the river tell geologists a lot about Earth's history.

The Grand Canyon is:

446 km long

Up to 29 km wide

1,857 m deep

At its deepest point, the Grand Canyon could fit four Empire State buildings stacked on top of each other!

Coastal Erosion

As well as rivers, the ocean can also cause the land to erode. This is called coastal erosion. Areas of land that stick out into the sea, called headlands, are the most vulnerable and can form interesting features such as:

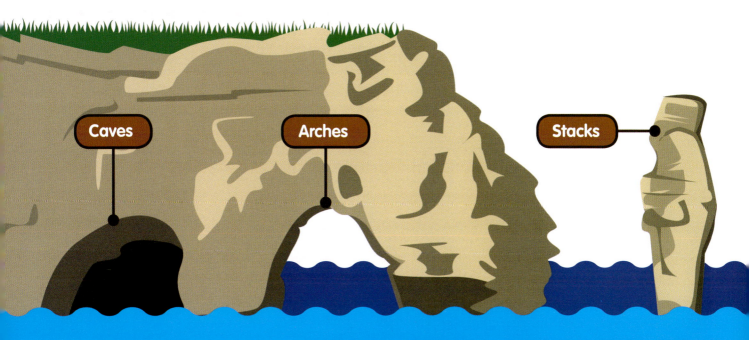

Caves form when waves crash against cracks in a cliff face. The water in waves contains grains of sand and other materials that help wear away the land.

When the cave is formed in a headland it might be eroded all the way through to the other side, forming an **arch**.

Stacks form when the arch becomes too wide to support itself and the top collapses into the sea.

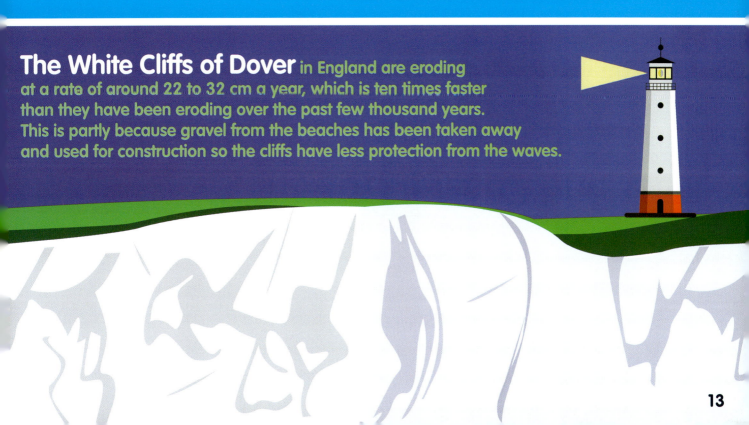

The White Cliffs of Dover in England are eroding at a rate of around 22 to 32 cm a year, which is ten times faster than they have been eroding over the past few thousand years. This is partly because gravel from the beaches has been taken away and used for construction so the cliffs have less protection from the waves.

Rock and Crystal Structures

Rocks

Rocks are made of tiny pieces of minerals called grains, which fit together. Whether a rock is hard or soft, porous or nonporous depends on the size and shape of its grains.

Rock grains come in all different shapes, sizes and colours depending on how the rock is formed.

Water Flow

Some rocks have grains that are interlocking and fit together tightly. These rocks are usually hard and don't let much water in. They are nonporous.

Granite has interlocking grains. It is hard and nonporous.

Some rocks have rounded grains that have gaps between them. They are usually softer and more porous.

Sandstone has rounded grains. It is soft and porous.

Crystals

The grains in igneous rocks are often crystals. The interlocking grains in granite are made from crystals that are formed as magma cools slowly underground.

Granite in the Earth's Crust

Other Rocks in the Earth's Crust

Granite makes up 70–80% of the Earth's crust.

Granite contains the crystals of four minerals:

 Quartz

 Feldspar

Mica

 Hornblende

Granite is **25%** Quartz.

Crystals can be very small or incredibly big. The Giant Crystal Cave in Mexico contains crystals that weigh 55,000 kilograms (kg). That's about the same weight as 110 grand pianos!

 = 22 Pianos

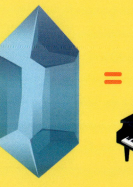 =

Crystals in the Giant Crystal Cave can reach up to **11 m** in length! This is about as tall as a telephone pole.

Crystals

Different minerals form different shapes when they grow, leading to many different types of crystal. Crystals tend to form in six main shapes, called systems.

Hexagonal

Hexagonal crystals are shaped like hexagonal <u>prisms</u>.

Quartz

Triclinic

Triclinic crystals can have strange shapes. They are usually flat with sharp edges.

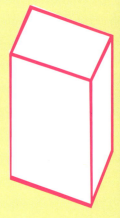

Turquoise

Cubic

Cubic crystals are shaped like blocks.

Diamond

Monoclinic

Monoclinic crystals have sides of unequal lengths and often have a pyramid at the end.

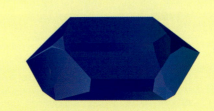

Azurite

Orthorhombic

Orthorhombic crystals are short and stubby like sticks.

Topaz

Tetragonal

Tetragonal systems are long crystals with four sides. They might have pyramid shapes at each end.

Rutile

Crystal systems <u>classify</u> the way that single minerals grow into crystals, but crystals tend to grow together forming a pattern. We call these patterns crystal habits.

Here are some crystal habits you are likely to come across if you see crystals in a museum.

Acicular

This crystal habit is spiky and the crystals grow like needles.

Cubic

These crystals grow like stacked up cubes.

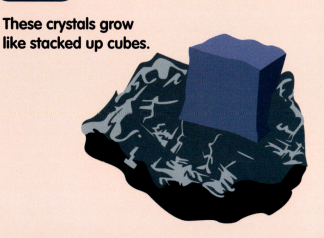

Botryoidal/Globular

The crystals in this habit grow like bunches of grapes.

Filiform/Capillary

Crystals in this habit grow like very fine hair; they almost look furry.

Columnar

Crystals in this habit grow long, thin, and spiky.

Platy

A flat tablet-shaped crystal habit.

Diamonds

Diamonds are the hardest of all gemstones. They are made from the element carbon, which also makes graphite – the grey stuff in your pencil!

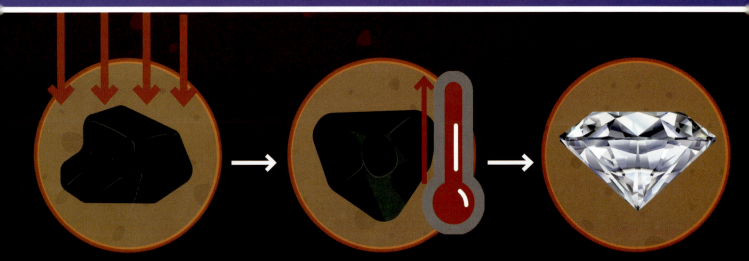

140–190 km underground in the Earth's mantle, carbon is under a huge amount of pressure.

The carbon is heated to temperatures of around **2,000 degrees Celsius.**

This heat and pressure changes the structure of the atoms in the carbon, turning it into diamond.

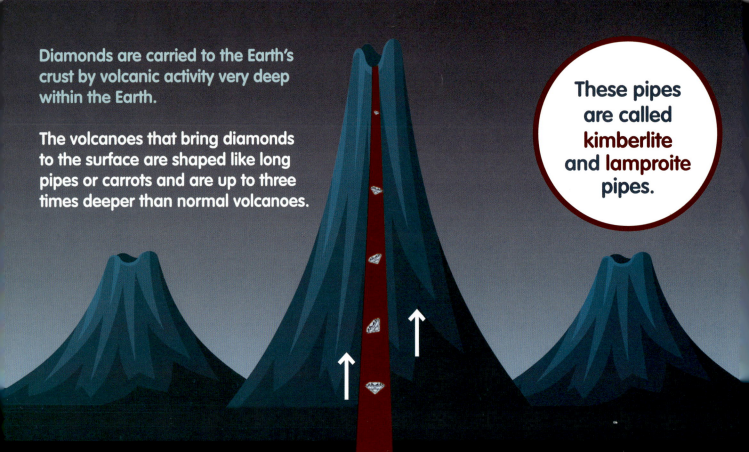

Diamonds are carried to the Earth's crust by volcanic activity very deep within the Earth.

The volcanoes that bring diamonds to the surface are shaped like long pipes or carrots and are up to three times deeper than normal volcanoes.

These pipes are called **kimberlite** and **lamproite** pipes.

Only 1 in 200 volcanic pipes contain gem-quality diamonds.

= 25 Volcanic Pipes

Carbon comes in many different forms depending on the structure of its atoms.

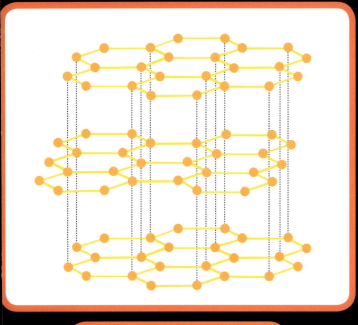

Structure of Carbon in Graphite

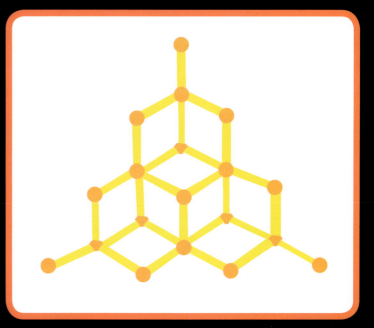

Structure of Carbon in Diamond

Lots of people think that diamonds are formed from coal because they are both made of carbon, but this is not true. Geologists think diamonds are made from carbon trapped in the Earth from when the planet was first formed around 4.6 billion years ago.

The Cullinan Diamond is the largest gem-quality rough diamond ever found.

It was cut into nine major stones, the largest of which is mounted in the Sovereign's Sceptre which is part of the **British Crown Jewels.**

Gemstones

Gems, or gemstones, are precious or semi-precious stones made of rare pieces of minerals that are found underground. Some gems, like diamonds and amethysts, are crystals but some, like amber and opal, are not. Because they are usually brightly coloured and patterned, gemstones are used for jewellery or for decoration.

Some gems aren't stones at all but are actually made from <u>organic</u> materials.

Jet is a black gemstone made from decaying wood that has been put under extreme pressure.

Opal is formed from water picking up silica from sandstone as it trickles through the earth.

Jet

Opal

Diamond

Rose Quartz

Sapphire

Tiger's Eye

Ruby

Topaz

Amber is a gem used in jewellery that is made from <u>fossilised</u> tree <u>resin</u>. Sometimes insects and other creatures get trapped in tree resin, so amber often contains fossilised insects.

Things that have been fossilised in amber include:

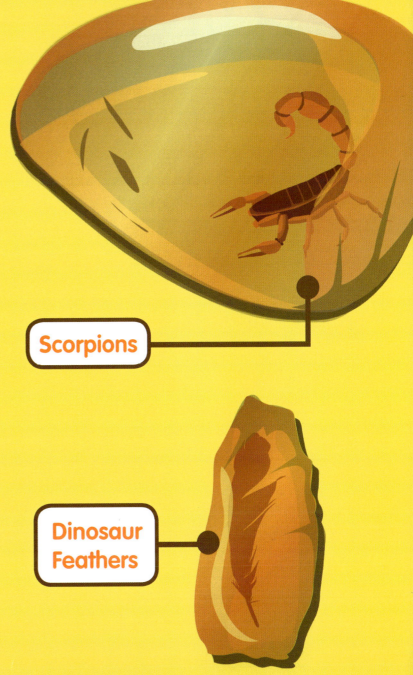

Scorpions

Dinosaur Feathers

99-Million-Year-Old Ants

Pearls are made by oysters. Oysters produce a shiny substance called nacre. When an oyster gets something small, like a grain of sand, caught in its shell, it covers it in layers of nacre which eventually form a shiny pearl.

The biggest pearl ever found is 67 cm long and weighs 34 kg, which is about as much as an Afghan hound.

Fossils

Fossils are the remains of plants and animals that died a long time ago and became <u>preserved</u> in rocks.

These plants and animals would get trapped in sediment and then buried under layers of rock for years and years turning both the thing itself and the layers around it into solid rock.

There are four main types of fossil:

Mould fossils – These are impressions (shapes) left behind in the rock after the animal or plant <u>decomposes</u>.

Trace Fossils – These are marks that an animal or plant has left behind that has made an impression. Footprints or imprints of nests are trace fossils.

Cast Fossils – These are when the plant or animal decomposes but the impressions left behind are filled in, creating a <u>3D</u> image of the living thing instead of just an indent.

True-Form Fossils – These fossils are the actual remains of a living thing that have been preserved, often by getting caught in ice or tree resin. Dinosaur skeletons are a type of true-form fossil.

Fossils Around The World

Fossils can be found all around the world. Some of the best places for finding fossils are:

Jurassic Coast, England
Dinosaurs and ammonites
(a type of prehistoric sea creature)
have been uncovered here.

Stránská Skála, Czech Republic
The remains of homotherium, a type of
sabre-toothed cat, have been found here.

Jiufotang Formation, China
Prehistoric birds, feathered dinosaurs
and pterosaurs have been found here.

Ediacara Hills, Australia
Excavations in this area uncovered
550-million-year old jellyfish fossils.

One of the largest dinosaur
footprint fossils ever found
is **1.7 m long.** That's about the
same length as a whole person!

Ancient Stones

Rocks and stones can tell us a lot about creatures that walked the Earth before human beings, but they can also tell us a lot about human history. Rocks and gems have been used by humans for buildings, tools, decoration and religion for thousands of years.

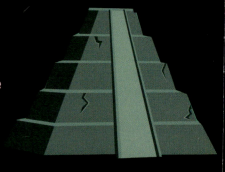

Stonehenge

Stonehenge is a famous prehistoric <u>monument</u> found in Salisbury, England.

It is made of two types of stone: bluestone, which makes up the inner circle of stones, and sarsen sandstone, which makes up the much older outer circle. The bluestone was transported over 200 km all the way from Wales.

Out of **85** sarsen stones used to build Stonehenge, only **53** remain.

Easter Island

Easter Island is famous for its stone monuments called moai or 'Easter Island heads' <u>erected</u> by the Rapa Nui people who inhabited the island.

10 m tall!

x43

87 tonnes – that's about the same as 43 saloon cars!

The monuments have large heads, small bodies and long noses, and <u>archaeologists</u> believe they were built to represent the <u>ancestors</u> of the Rapa Nui people.

The biggest monument weighs around 87 tonnes, so how the rocks were moved by the Rapa Nui people without modern technology is mostly a mystery to archaeologists. They believe the monuments might have been held upright in ropes and 'walked' by shuffling them forwards and side-to-side.

Basalt – 13

Red Scoria – 17

Trachyte – 22

The moai are made from many different types of rock:

Tuff – 847

Art With Rocks

Terracotta Army

Lots of amazing art, such as buildings and sculptures, have been made using rocks.

The Terracotta Army in Shaanxi, China is a collection of thousands of statues built to represent the army of Qin Shi Huang, the first emperor of China. The statues are made out of terracotta which is made by heating clay – a sedimentary rock made of very fine grains. Clay is a very mouldable rock when used with water.

The statues were buried with the emperor around 210–209 BC because it was thought they would protect him in the afterlife.

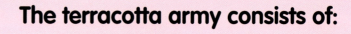

The terracotta army consists of:

150 Chariots

520 Horses

150 Cavalry Horses

8,000 Soldiers

The statues were buried in giant pits, the biggest of which is the size of almost three football pitches!

Marble Statues

Many famous sculptures are made from the **metamorphic rock, marble**. It is made of medium-sized interlocking grains made of calcite crystals.

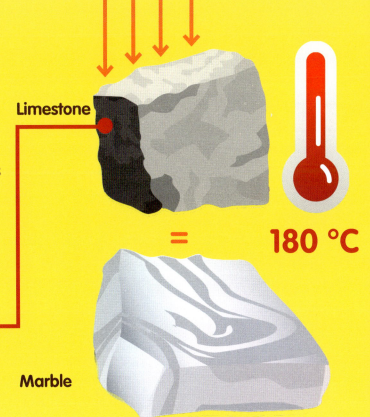

Limestone

= 180 °C

Marble

Marble forms when limestone is exposed to high pressure and temperature. Marble has much finer grains than limestone which means that sculptors can add much finer detail when making a statue.

Carrara marble is a type of white or blue-grey marble that comes from a quarry in Carrara in Tuscany, Italy.

Some of the most famous marble architecture and sculptures were made from Carrara marble including:

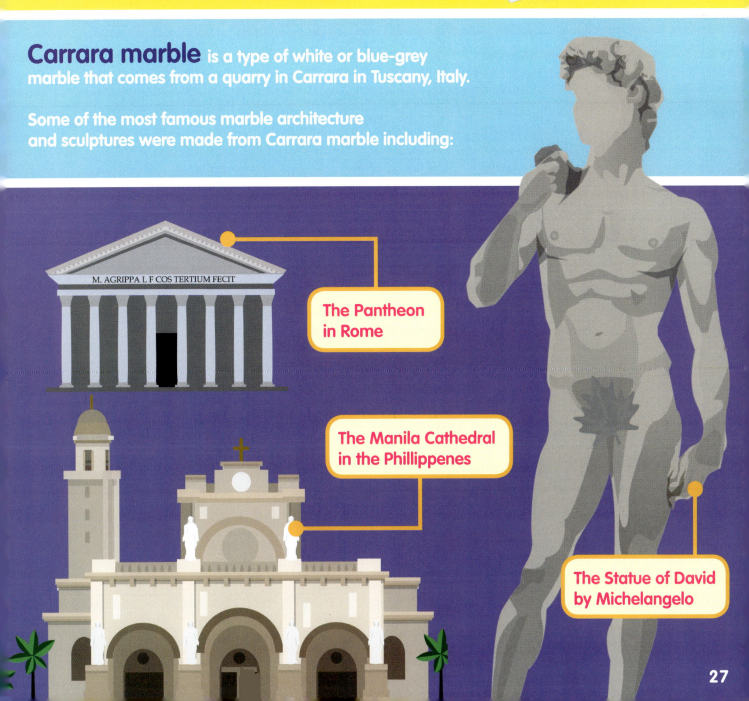

M. AGRIPPA L F COS TERTIUM FECIT

The Pantheon in Rome

The Manila Cathedral in the Phillippenes

The Statue of David by Michelangelo

Jewellery

Jewellery-making is also an art form. Jewellery makers are called jewellers and they make things like rings, bracelets, pendants, earrings and much more, using gemstones and metals like gold and silver.

Gold and silver are both metals that are found in the Earth's crust and are very rare.

24 carat gold is the purest and most expensive kind of gold but it is not used in jewellery because it is too soft. Instead it is mixed with other metals such as copper and silver.

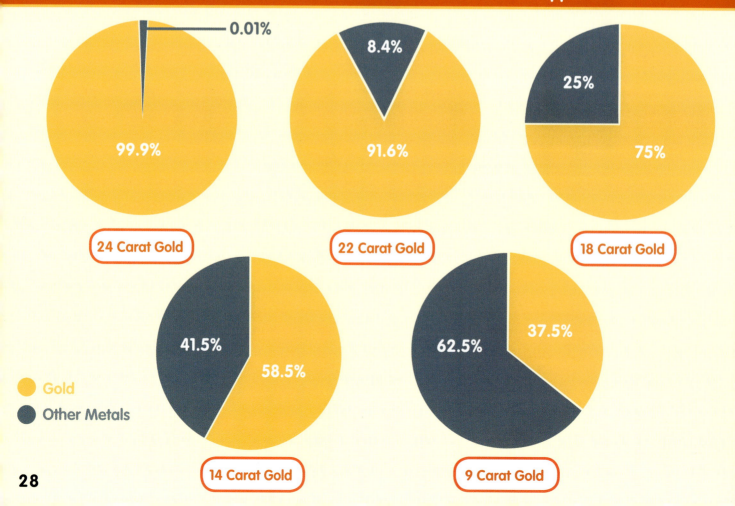

0.01%

99.9%

24 Carat Gold

8.4%

91.6%

22 Carat Gold

25%

75%

18 Carat Gold

41.5%

58.5%

14 Carat Gold

62.5%

37.5%

9 Carat Gold

● Gold
● Other Metals

Birthstones

Birthstones are gemstones which are connected to different months of the year. The idea of birthstones is thought to be an ancient one and possibly came about from a story in the Bible where Aaron, the High Priest of the Hebrews, is given a <u>breastplate</u> with 12 gemstones on it, representing the 12 tribes of Israel. In modern times 12 gemstones are used to represent the 12 months of the year.

A person's birthstone is the stone connected to the month they were born in. What is your birthstone?

Activity

Using the birthstone chart on page 29, why not find out as much as you can about your birthstone?

Here are some questions that you could find out the answers to:

1. How is your birthstone formed?

2. Where is your birthstone most commonly found?

3. Is your birthstone a crystal?

4. If your birthstone is made underground, how deep underground is it formed?

5. How rare is your birthstone?

Glossary

3D	an object which has height, width and depth
acidic	contains a chemical substance that causes damage to the natural environment
ancestors	persons from whom one is descended, for example a great-grandparent
archaeologists	historians who study buried ruins and ancient objects in order to learn about human history
architecture	style or way of building
atoms	the smallest part of a chemical element, which is made up of even smaller particles
breastplate	a piece of armour covering the chest
canyon	a large valley with steep sides and a river flowing through it
cavalry	the part of an army that serve on horseback
classify	to arrange things into groups based on shared characteristics
compaction	the process by which pressure put on sediment causes it to stick together and form rock
decomposes	decays or rots
deposited	to leave something somewhere
element	a pure substance made from only one type of atom
erected	built or put together then set upright
fossilised	an animal or plant that has been preserved for so long that it has become a fossil
liquefied	to be made liquid
monument	buildings or structures that are of historical interest or importance
organic	made of living matter
preserved	maintained in its original or current state
prisms	objects with flat sides and two identical ends
resin	a gummy substance made by trees
solidifies	make or become solid
transformation	a change in form, nature, or appearance

Index

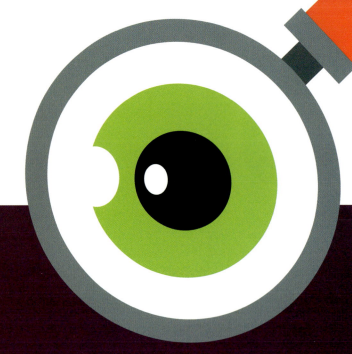

atoms 18–19

birthstones 29–30

bluestone 24

carbon 18–19

Carrara marble 27

caves 10–11, 13, 15

crust 4–5, 9, 15, 18, 28

crystal
-habits 17
-systems 16–17

Cullinan Diamond, The 19

diamonds 16, 18–20, 29

erosion 6, 9–10, 12–13

fossils 21–23

Giant Crystal Cave, The 15

Giant's Causeway, The 8

gold 28

grains 6, 13–15, 26–27

Grand Canyon, The 12

granite 4, 8, 14–15

heat 7, 9, 18, 26

igneous 6, 8–9, 15

lava 8

limestone 6, 10, 27

magma 4–5, 7–9, 15

mantle 4, 18

marble 7, 27

metamorphic 6–7, 9, 27

moai 25

nonporous 14

porous 10, 14

pressure 7, 9, 18, 20, 27

rock cycle, the 9

sandstone 6, 14, 20, 24

sedimentary 6, 9–10, 26

silver 28

Stonehenge 24

Taj Mahal 7

tectonic plates 5

Terracotta Army 26

volcanoes 8–9, 18–19

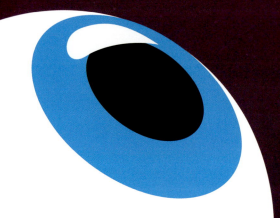